WALKING
the
RIDGES & RIGGS

of the

NORTH YORK MOORS

by

J.Brian Beadle

First published in Great Britain in 1997 by Trailblazer Publishing (Scarborough)

ISBN 1 899004 17 3

Trailblazer Publishing (Scarborough)
Stoneways
South End
Burniston
Scarborough. YO13 0HP

MAPS

The maps in this book are not to scale and are for guidance only. They do not accurately portray the right of way. It is the readers responsibility not to stray from the right of way and it is strongly advised that you take an Ordnance Survey map with you on the walk.

WARNING

Whilst every effort has been made for accuracy neither the publisher nor the author bear responsibility for the alteration, closure or portrayal of rights of way in this book. It is the readers responsibility not to invade private land or stray from the public right of way. All routes in the book should be treated with respect and all precautions taken before setting out. Take food, drink, an emergency whistle and warm clothing with you and tell someone where you are going and your expected time of return. Any person using information in this book does so at their own risk.

CONTENTS

A TRAVERSE OF GLAISDALE RIGG

Glaisdale is without doubt one of the prettiest dales on the North York Moors. To appreciate it fully this walk takes you onto Glaisdale Rigg, with its marker stones, old sign post and iron workings. Then for contrast it returns on the opposite side giving a totally different aspect to this lush, green dale. If you visit Beggars Bridge, a good example of an ancient packhorse bridge, take some of the local butcher's pies with you, they are magnificent!

THE HISTORY

Beggars Bridge at Glaisdale is another fine packhorse bridge in beautiful Eskdale. Built it is believed by Thomas Ferries in the 17th century. He was a poor farm worker and was not allowed to marry his love until he became rich. He decided to go away to make his fortune but before departing he went to see his lover but could not cross the River Esk whilst in flood. He vowed to return and build a bridge. He fought alongside Drake in the Armada then made a huge fortune plundering the Spanish. He returned to Glaisdale to claim his girl, married her and went to live in Hull where he became Sheriff. Oh yes, he did build the bridge over the River Esk which we can still see today. Glaisdale was mentioned in the doomsday book, and in the 18th century iron works were started nearby with three furnaces and a 250ft chimney. Population increased from around 600 to 2000. The 18th century houses can still to be seen today. Many shafts were sunk and ore taken away on the railway. However the project soon foundered and the land returned to farming.

INFORMATION

Distance - 7 miles, 8½ miles if Beggars Bridge visited
Time - 3 or 4 hours
Map - OS Landranger 94. OS Outdoor Leisure 27
Start - Glaisdale, GR 775054
Terrain - Moorland bridleways and farm tracks
Parking - Street parking in the village
Refreshments - The Mitre Tavern (recommended), and Frosts
Butcher's Shop for delicious pies. Both are in Glaisdale village.

BOOTS ON!

Leave Glaisdale in a westerly direction towards Lealholm. On the edge of the village at High Leas Farm turn left onto a wide bridleway. This takes you through a gate and climbs onto Glaisdale Moor. Keep straight on at all times to eventually meet a wide farm track. Turn right here then in about fifty yards turn left onto a bridleway. The track falls downhill soon and when you meet a wide track go right climbing up again onto the moor. Where the track forks, keep right. At the top of the hill you meet another wide track, turn left onto it then shortly right at a junction of wide tracks. This climbs over Glaisdale Rigg to meet a road. Turn left, then immediately left again onto a bridleway through the heather to soon meet a wide track. Cross the track to follow the bridleway opposite then down the hill to exit onto the road in the dale bottom. Turn left here then at the entrance to Plum Tree Farm turn right along the farm driveway signed as a bridleway. Go straight on through the farmyard, through a gate and onto a wide track. Soon bear left across a pretty bridge then follow the blue waymarks passing over stiles and through gates which are all waymarked. Eventually you meet the road at the entrance to a farm. Go left along the road and in about ½ mile at the entrance to Bank House Farm go right onto the farm track following the bridleway sign. At the next farm take the blue waymark to the right through the farmyard and exit through a small gate. Follow the blue waymarks which lead eventually into a copse. Exit the copse into a field, then through a gate. Keep straight ahead now to the opposite hedge choosing your way through it then head slightly left towards a large wooden building. Go through the gate then left downhill to a bridleway signpost. Go right here to a gate. Do not go through the gate but turn right towards the Oak tree then left through a small gate. Down to the river now and over a bridge then through a gate onto a paved track. Left at the end as waymarked then follow the signs along a wide track, across a field and eventually the road. Turn right to return to Glaisdale village. To visit Beggars Bridge pass through the village towards Egton passing numerous pubs and the station tea rooms. When the road falls steeply Beggars Bridge is on your right. Unfortunately you will have to return the same way.

ROUTE 2
RUDLAND RIGG

Dividing the valleys of Bransdale and Farndale is the dominant ridge of Rudland Rigg. The high track over the top of the Rigg played its part in the industrial heritage of the area when ironstone mining was prominent. We reach the Rigg from Low Mill, a tiny community at the start of the daffodil valley of Farndale. This walk links the lush farmland of the sheltered valleys to the bleak nakedness of the Rigg with incredible scenery along the way.

THE HISTORY

Rudland Rigg was part of an ancient highway between Kirkbymoorside and Stokesley. Not only cattle drovers used the route but waggoners buying and selling farm produce to and from the markets were still using the road in the early 1900's. The road from the village of Fadmoor to Rudland Rigg was called Waingate which is Anglo Saxon for waggon road. The surface over the Rigg is a good example of a medieval road being in much the same condition now as it was a hundred years ago.

Along the Rigg is to be found a huge stone, the 'Gammon Stone' which leans to one side. On that side is an inscription in Hebrew which means Hallelujah. The work is credited to the Reverend Strickland a local clergyman. The whole area around the Rigg was used for mining and half way along the Rigg is a crossing, Bloworth Crossing, where the mineral railway carried ore from the Rosedale and Farndale mines on its way to Teesside. The area of and surrounding Rudland Rigg was a busy industrial complex in the boom days of the 19th century.

INFORMATION

Distance -12½ miles (20km)
Time - 5 hours
Map - OS Landranger 100, OS Outdoor Leisure 26
Start - Lowna, GR 686910. Small car park
Terrain - Rough moorland paths and grassy bridleways
Parking - Small car park at Lowna
Refreshment - Sandwiches & flask this time!

STRETCH THOSE LEGS!

Start from the small car park at Lowna. There is parking here for eight cars so be early. Leave on the path at the rear of the car park and soon you will arrive

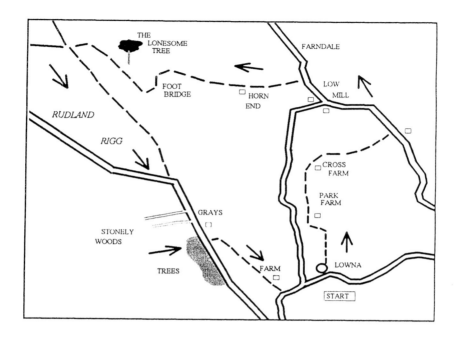

at a footbridge over the River Dove. Turn right over the bridge then left at the sign for Low Mill via Park Farm. Not far along the path take a detour to the left to visit the ancient Lowna burial ground. The track winds its way through the summer bracken to eventually arrive at a small gate, turn right following the footpath sign and at the bottom of the hill go left at a junction of footpaths. After struggling through a 'jungle path' you come to a small metal gate. Go sharp left here up the hill. At the top of the hill cross the stile on the left. It is a bit tricky now as the path is undefined in the heather, but if you follow in the direction of the arrow and climb the hill diagonally to the right you will meet a fence at the top. If you can't see the next stile follow the fence to the right and you won't miss it. Cross the stile and the wide track in front of you and continue straight ahead through the heather to arrive at the road to Park Farm in a few yards. At the farm pass through the farmyard, the dogs bark but are seemingly friendly. After leaving the farmyard follow the waymark to the left and exit the field by the gate. Continue straight ahead, through another gate and soon you will arrive at Cross Farm.

Go slightly right here to find a yellow waymark on the farm gate leading to a field. Turn right in the field and look for a stile hidden in the hedge opposite down the hill. Follow the waymarked stiles down the hill to eventually arrive at a footbridge across the River Dove. Turn sharp left along the river bank after the bridge and after crossing more stiles and another footbridge turn right keeping the river on your right to exit the field by a gate and along a lane to the road. Left at the road then left again at the sign for Low Mill. At Low Mill turn right and in half a mile turn left along the road to Horn End signed as a bridleway to Rudland Rigg. After the farm enter a field, take care there might the local Bull roaming with his concubines, and follow the path and waymarks which lead to a footbridge in about half a mile.

Cross the bridge and keep to the left following the line of the wall to a stile. Over the stile go diagonally uphill to the right following a worn track which soon bends sharp right and heads ever onwards and upwards through heather and bracken with confirmation waymarks along the way. When you reach a lonesome tree the path becomes undefined for a few yards. Keep right past the tree and you will soon pick up the path again heading uphill to the left. Climbing now past the shooting butts the path opens out to reach the wide track across Rudland Rigg. Left here to enjoy the delights of walking over the Rigg to reach the Bransdale road in about three miles. Continue straight ahead towards Gillamoor and in one mile at the start of a steep hill just past a farm on the left turn left at the bridleway sign into a field. Keep close to the left here and at the next gate do not pass through but turn sharp right along a wide bridleway. Keep straight on at all times eventually passing through a farmyard to follow the farm driveway to the road. Turn left at the road to take you back to the car park at Lowna.

- - - o 0 o - - -

ROUTE 3

NORTHDALE RIGG

Northdale Rigg protects Rosedale from the severe north east winds. We cross the Rigg on our way to an old mining area before walking over the wild Hamer Moor to head back to the shelter of the dale. The views across the dale to Spaunton Moor and Rosedale Bank Top are outstanding.

THE HISTORY

Look out for the industrial heritage as you walk the moors, especially on Hamer Moor where there are numerous old workings. The Romans were around here, in fact a hoard of 3rd century coins were found at Hamer House. On the return journey look across the valley to the old kilns on the opposite side. Today,

Rosedale's economy thrives on tourism and farming. But the area has been host to many industries in the past. The Romans brought weaving and pottery and the Cistercians built their Priory. The ironstone industry was rife as industrial Teesside expanded rapidly and became hungry for raw materials. The French even made glass here in the 16th century! But what of the Abbey? All that remains is a buttressed turret which can be found in the village. If you stand with your back to the public conveniences near the Milburn Arms and look over the wall opposite you will see the turret across the field. Other remains will be found in the stonework of local houses. The Abbey was a Priory of the Cistercian order with nine nuns and a Prioress. There were a few lay workers mainly farmers and shepherds. The Priory sometimes had twelve sacks of wool for sale annually taken from their large flocks of sheep on the moors. In 1322 the Scots raided Rosedale and severely damaged the Priory, so much so that the nuns were rehabilitated elsewhere until repairs were carried out. It was occupied until Henry 8th called for the suppression of the monasteries in 1535 and the priory was destroyed.

INFORMATION

Distance - 8 miles (13 km).
Time - 3½ hours.
Maps - OS Landranger 100.
Start - Rosedale Abbey, GR 725960
Terrain - Moorland paths. Undefined in places over Rigg
Refreshment - Two cafes and two pubs in Rosedale Abbey

PULL YOUR SOCKS UP!

Start from the small car park behind the Milburn Arms. If full there is another park adjacent to the pub. Follow the public footpath sign through the gate at the rear of the car park. Cross the field staying close to Northdale Beck on your left. Keep following the beck crossing several stiles on the way until you arrive at a signpost. Continue straight ahead here following the sign for 'concessionary path'. The path follows the river then after two more stiles you reach a bridge and a gate to a signpost. Keep straight on still following the bridleway sign. At the road turn right and in about half a mile immediately after a house used as a stable, turn right through a gate at the bridleway sign. Go uphill to climb onto the moor via a gate. Take the left fork now and still climbing head for another gate onto open moorland. Soon you cross a wide track but keep on your narrow path through the heather. The track becomes undefined at times, even disappearing altogether. If you head for the shooting butts slightly to your left you will come to a crevice, keep right here and follow

9

the crevice which in winter could be wet. This takes you downhill to a small stream. On the horizon straight ahead you will see mounds of the old workings. This is where you are heading. Cross the stream and you should see a narrow path winding its way through the heather. Follow the line of the wall on the right and when the wall bends to the right keep straight ahead to pass through the middle of the workings. The track then bears right to the road. Cross the road taking the bridleway sign. The wide track soon forks, take the right fork away from the wall. Now for the tricky bit! In about a mile you will pass a pile of stones on the right. Then, in a hundred yards or so look for a wide swathe of grass through the heather leading to a gate in the wall on your right. If you reach a clump of trees on the right you have gone too far and are trespassing. You must turn right before the small plantation! Pass through the gate in the wall and across a couple of fields to reach a quiet road at the side of a farm. Turn right here and walk along the road for about a mile where at a junction near a derelict farmhouse keep straight ahead, then in a few yards turn right at the public footpath sign. This leads through a pleasant wood rich in bilberries. Follow the obvious path along the edge of the wood and onto the moor, crossing two stiles and a gate. At the road cross a stone stile and turn right then immediately left at the footpath sign. It is downhill now with scintillating views across Rosedale to the old mine workings on the other side of the valley. Pass through a gate and over a stile to arrive at a signpost. Turn right eventually passing over a large stile on the way to a farm. Go through the farm gate then left to exit onto the road. Follow the minor road to the junction and turn right to head back to Rosedale and the welcoming Milburn Arms

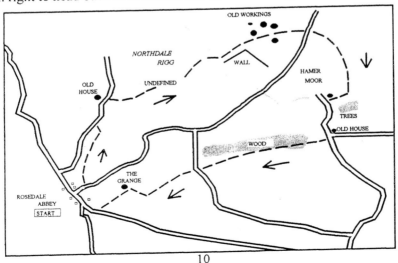

ROUTE 4
BROXA RIGG

Broxa Rigg is a peninsular of land which separates the tiny valley of Low Dales with the beautiful valley of Hackness and the River Derwent. As we walk down the end of the Rigg the lake and parkland of Hackness Hall astounds us with its magnificence.

THE HISTORY

The ancient village of Hackness lies in a tranquil valley surrounded by wooded hills. It boasts a fine church which has several Norman arches. Early in the 7th century Hilda, founder of Whitby Abbey, set up a monastic cell at Hackness with nuns from Whitby. The story goes that when Hilda died she appeared to the nuns at Hackness who saw her ascending to heaven. The monastery closed when it was sacked by the Danes.

After the Norman Conquest in 1078 a Benedictine monastery was built. In fact there may have been two monastic churches at Hackness at one time according to the Domesday Book. The Monks lived a full life at Hackness and even manufactured iron nearby in Forge Valley. Their monastery lasted until the dissolution. Religious worship is catered for today at Hackness by a church with many interesting relics inside, including fragments of a cross which is believed to have been part of the old monastery.

Near the church is Hackness Hall, the seat of Lord Derwent. The famous diarist Lady Holby having lived there previously. The grounds of the Hall are a pleasure which is matched by the view across the lake from the front of the Hall. The gardens are usually open once each year in the summer months.

INFORMATION

Distance - 7 miles (11km)
Time - 3 hours
Maps - OS Landranger 101, Outdoor Leisure 27
Start - Lowdales/Highdales road end, Hackness. GR 969906
Terrain: Mainly grassy tracks, rough in places
Parking - Roadside at Hackness
Refreshments: The Moorcock Inn at Langdale End

WATERPROOFS ON!

The walk starts at the junction of the road to Low Dales/High Dales adjacent to the bridge over the beck in Hackness village. Walk through the village over the bridge, past the school, post office and church. After passing under a fine bridge look for the ice-house in the wood on the left. Continue along until you arrive at a group of public footpath signs. Take the one on the right to do a 'u' turn and walk along a path through the trees close to the fence on your left. This path leads to a stile into a meadow, follow the waymarks across the grass as you pass behind the Hall and lake. Eventually you will see a stile in the middle of a fence crossing the field. Follow the waymarks behind Mill Farm then drop down to the road over a stile in the hedge. Cross the road diagonally left then turn right at the footpath sign and over the bridge across the River Derwent and into a field leading to the tiny village of Wrench Green. Keep straight ahead to join a tarmac road then straight on up the hill following the

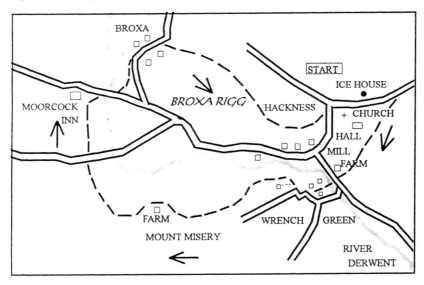

link sign for Cockmoor Hall. At the entrance to Slack Farm follow the footpath sign along the farm road. In a few hundred yards go right at the waymark up the hill. Keep following these waymarks round to the left then into a copse of trees to go right. At the end of the trees keep straight on through the gorse bushes and over the hill bearing slightly left. Look out for the next waymark and a stile then down the hill and right through a small gate following the yellow arrow into a wood. Through the trees now to exit at the farm. This high ground is called Mount Misery and offers good views across to Troutsdale. Keeping the farm on your left follow the fence round to the left. Once past the farm go straight on and over a stile through the hedge, down an overgrown path and onto a farm road. Turn right onto the road and follow it all the way without deviation onto the tarmac road. Take the public bridleway opposite and climb up the hill following a wide track. At a small gate the route splits. Keep right here along the edge of the field following the arrow. The path soon crosses a stile into route splits. Keep right here along the edge of the field following the arrow. The path soon crosses a stile into a field then heads diagonally right to another stile in the hedge. Bear left over the stile and head down through the bracken eventually reaching a stone bridge on the right. Cross the bridge to take you past the farm to the road. Turn left here up the hill if you would like to take some refreshment at the Moorcock Inn. When you can drag yourself away from the superb ale retrace your steps back to the farm past the church and follow the road to a bridge over the River Derwent. Immediately after the bridge cross the stile into a field on the left. Turn immediately right and go straight up the bank side on a sometimes undefined path. Half way up you will meet a wide bridleway, turn left onto it to continue to the top of the hill and exit onto the road through a gate.

Go left now into Broxa village. At the end of the village where the road narrows follow the footpath sign to the right along a wide track. In a few yards go straight ahead and cross a stile into a field. Follow the track and its waymarks over several stiles and fields. After five stiles and one fence you are nearing the end of this peninsula of land. Keep to the right near the trees now and look for an obvious wide track leading through a gate downhill. At the road turn left to return to your transport.

- - - o 0 o - - -

ROUTE 5

LANGDALE RIGG & MAW RIGG

Langdale End consists of a few houses and farms, a church and an interesting old Inn. Peacefully situated amongst odd shaped hills the village has not changed much in a hundred years, apart from the Moorcock Inn. Once, as the sign above the door still proclaims, it had a 6 day license. It was tastefully restored only a few years ago keeping many of the old features intact. Beer is now pulled instead of being served in a jug! Try the Inn at the end of your walk but if you are relying on it being open it would be best to ring them the day before to ensure that they will be open!

THE HISTORY

Langdale End is surrounded by hill and moor. Peaceful valleys, the silence broken by the occasional bark of a tiresome dog. Iron stained becks rush through the forests from the moors and Riggs to end up in the mighty River Derwent, whose source is at High Woof Howe - on the opposite ridge to Langdale Rigg. Odd shaped hills present themselves, the two 'sugar loaves', Howden Hill at the Rigg end and Blakey Topping in the far distance complement this area of outstanding beauty which the Victorians called 'Little Switzerland'. Agriculture and forestry play a big part in the dale but as a contrast there is an outdoor pursuit centre situated in Langdale Forest.

INFORMATION

Distance - 7 miles (11Km)

Time - 3 hours

Map - OS Landranger 101, OS Outdoor Leisure 27

Start - Langdale End, GR 939913

Terrain - Wide grassy path across the Rigg. Forest roads and tracks

Parking - Near the telephone box otherwise on the grass verge near the bridge

Refreshment - The Moorcock Inn at Langdale End. (01723 882268)

ASCEND THAT RIGG!

Set off past the Moorcock Inn and then in a few hundred yards turn right along a narrow road following the sign to Birch Hall. In about 400 yards turn right

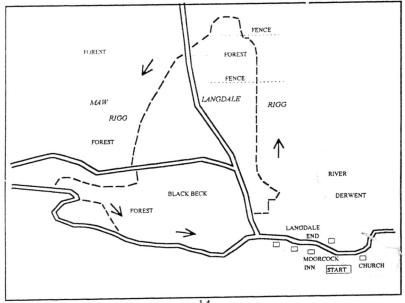

over a stile at the public footpath sign. Turn left before the hedge and at the rtop of the field go right through the gate on the right. Turn left through the gate then right onto a wide track. Soon, turn left off the wide track towards the Rigg end onto another wide track. Walk straight on along the ridge making for the forest in the distance. There are good views towards Bickley and Blakey Topping from here.

Continue along the for almost a mile then keeping straight ahead cross a stile into the forest. The road is straight through the forest being nearly a mile along the Rigg, eventually cross a stile into a field. Aim diagonally left here to the corner of the field and cross a stile to turn immediately right onto a down-hill forest road . Before the bottom of the hill go left through the trees at the blue man waymark. Continue through the forest crossing several forest roads following the blue man waymark.

Soon you arrive at a forest clearing and the bridge over Hipperley Beck, cross the bridge then continue along towards Maw Rigg end in front of you and climb across the Rigg. You now pick up a series of yellow waymarks and blue man waymarks which crosses more forest roads to soon reach the bank of Blue Beck. Turn right after the rhododendron bushes to climb to a small footbridge then follow the path down left again. Soon you arrive at the road, turn left here then uphill to a bend in the road. Take the path on the left now towards the forest where you see the Public Footpath sign and follow the yellow arrows. If in doubt bear right. The path eventually climbs back to the road. Turn left here for a scenic return to Langdale End and the Moorcock.

ROUTE 6
FOUR RIGGS AROUND GOATHLAND
Simon Howe Rigg, Two Howes Rigg, Moss Rigg and Wardle Rigg are traversed on this delightful walk. Also on route are a tarn, three howes and an ancient cross. What more could you ask for? A walk over open moorland and a stroll through the forest? You've got it!

THE HISTORY
Goathland, surrounded by high moorland where ancient settlements existed leaving many traces of entrenchments and man's existence. At Goathland village there was a hermitage which was an offshoot of St. Hilda's Abbey at Whitby. There are no remains but it is said to have been at the house called Abbots House.

Goathland is a superb place to stay for a walking or cycling holiday with easy access to the Moors and a Roman Road. The North Yorkshire Moors Railway from Pickering to Grosmont passes through the village stopping at Goathland Station. The railway is on the route of George Stephensons' original railway from Pickering to Whitby. The carriages in those days were copies of stagecoaches mounted on rolling stock to fit the rails and were pulled along by horses. The 1 in 5 incline from Beck Hole to Goathland was a serious problem for the railway and the coaches were hauled up using a metal wire which ingeniously used a system of water power to do the work. There were numerous accidents! Eventually the moors were blasted away to enable the line to take an easier route. The steam railway of today still takes the same route.

INFORMATION

Distance - 15 miles (24km)
Time - Enjoy the walk and take all day
Map - OS Landranger 94
OS Outdoor Leisure 27
Start - Goathland. GR 833013
Terrain - Moorland tracks
Parking - Car park in Goathland
Refreshments - Pubs and cafes in Goathland

PUT YOUR BEST FOOT FORWARD!

Start from the car park in Goathland and at the road turn right away from the Railway Station. Pass the Mallyan Spout Hotel turning right at the junction towards Egton Bridge. Shortly leave the road and turn left onto a signed bridleway heading up, and parallel to the road to a wooden sign for three bridleways. Go left here and climb to the ridge on an undefined path. Over the ridge there is a tarn on the right, keep left of the tarn on a wide track which climbs onto the moor to Moss Rigg and Two Howes Rigg. Keeping the howes on your left continue straight on heading towards Simon Howe on the horizon.

At Simon Howe go right along a track for 50yds then immediately sharp left onto a track through the heather. You will see some posts across the moor in the distance which will guide you past a sheep bield on your way to Wardle Green. The moor ends at Wardle Green crossing a beck and exiting through a gate then climbing a rocky ascent between the edge of the forest and a field. The route soon bears off to the right through a pair of old stone gateposts. Cross a field to a gate then diagonally right to another gate, eventually exiting

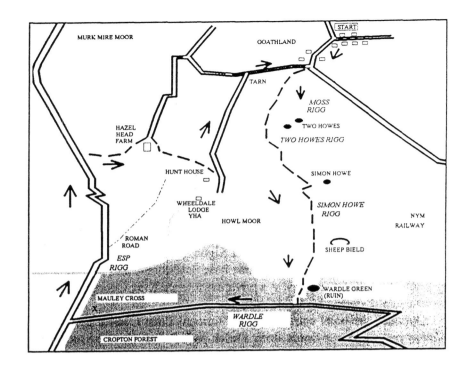

through yet another gate onto a forest road. Cross the forest road and ride straight ahead between the trees and a fence to the forest drive road and turn ight. Follow the forest drive for two miles until you meet another road. Turn right now onto the narrow road. In about four miles after the second set of double bends the road climbs, about a third of the way up the incline look for a wide track on your right, don't miss it. It is a sharp right turn onto the moor. The track goes round to a stile/gate then continues down to Hazel Head Farm on the right. Turn right through the farmyard, (please make sure to shut the gates), then continue straight ahead downhill through several gates to a stream Cross the stream, climb up passing through another gate then go right along an uphill track to the road. At the road go acute left then in one mile at the road junction turn right to return to Goathland.

- - - o 0 o - - -

ROUTE 7
THREE RIGGS FROM RAVENSCAR

The walk begins at Ravenscar which is perched on high cliffs which tower above the North Sea, it then heads off to traverses the moor to visit Lilla Cross. The approach is from the east over Shooting House Rigg and Blea Hill Rigg. The return from Lilla Cross is via Burn Howe Rigg to Jugger Howe and Ravenscar.

THE HISTORY

Historic Ravenscar is perched on the bleak 600ft high cliffs of Yorkshire's northern coast. Its heritage includes connections with royalty and the Roman Empire. Now, in less troubled times the great headland is owned by the National Trust for us all to enjoy. A mansion was built in 1774 on the highest point of the cliff on the site of a Roman Signal Station. It is now the Raven Hall Hotel which has an interesting nine hole golf course and a small swimming pool. When the mansion was a private residence King George 3rd would use it as a retreat during his bouts of madness.

Opposite the hotel entrance is the National Trust Coastal Centre. The bridleway past the centre heads along a brick paved road. On close scrutiny of the bricks you will find that they bear the name of the Ravenscar Brick Company. A few yards further along where the track narrows, turn left following the 'Trail' sign. After the bridge you soon arrive at the site of the old brickworks and an old alum quarry. All that remains now is a sheer cliff which forms an amphitheatre around the brickworks ruins. On a lower path are the remains of the alum works, once big business providing a dye fixer for the cloth trade.

INFORMATION

Distance - 16 miles (25km)
Time - 6 hours
Grading - Hard
Map - OS Landranger 94
OS Outdoor Leisure 27
Terrain - Fairly good coastal path
Start - Ravenscar. GR 981016
Refreshments - Tea shop at the old railway station, Ravenscar

RUCKSACK ON!

There is ample car parking along the approach road to Ravenscar. Start with the Raven Hall Hotel at your back and walk back along the road you arrived on. In about a quarter of a mile turn right at a bridleway sign along Robin Hood Lane. At the end of the road continue along a rough track following the bridleway sign. When the track forks go left, marked by a yellow waymark to

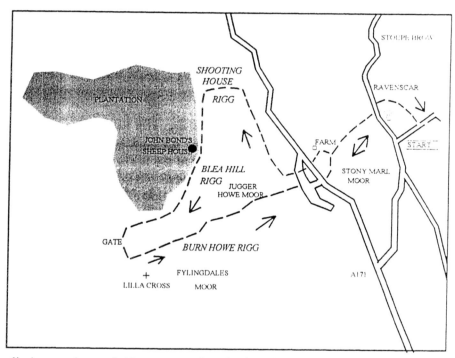

climb up to the road. Almost opposite take the bridleway signposted to Helwath. In one mile the track splits. Take the blue waymark arrow this time to the right leading to a farm road. Turn left and follow the bridleway sign. Cross the A171 and follow the public footpath sign to the old road opposite. Take the stile into the meadow as indicated by a yellow waymark. The oath takes down into Wragby Wood and a junction of streams; on the way keep the fence close on your right. Follow the path around to the right . When the path splits bear left then right over a wooden bridge. Follow the track to the right to eventually cross the beck. Keep following the beck as it twists and turns along the valley to cross Hollin Gill. Ignore the path along the gill and keep right still taking the line of Brown Rigg Beck. The path is undefined in places but keep near to the wall on the left. Passing some shooting huts and a house take the path to the right to join a chalk farm road. Soon leave the road turning left aiming for the corner of a wood and a yellow waymark. Cross two stiles then take the path to the left and head for a rickety gate into a wood.

Leave the wood by a stile onto a farm road. Head left over the bridge then immediately right onto a narrow path following the marshy beck. Keep close to the left hillside it is very boggy in the centre and must be avoided at all costs! After a hard, rough miles walking you meet a moorland road. Turn right aiming for a post in the distance then follow a trail sign left into a wood. Go left past the ruins of John Bond's Sheephouse along Sheephouse Rigg. In the wood keep the fence on the left then cross a stile onto the moor. At the beck keep to the track on the right. After a second beck crossing the track splits - go right.

This rough track climbs over the end of Blea Hill Rigg to Fylingdales Moor to a gate. Go through the gate then take the track to the left past the boundary stone and onto Burn Howe Rigg. On the horizon is Lilla Cross. When the track splits take the left fork then in about two miles descend into a lush green valley. Cross the footbridge over Jugger Howe Beck and follow the yellow waymark at first right then turn left and climb steeply up the end of Jugger Howe. The track soon joins a disused concrete army road to meet the A171. Cross to the path opposite and climb across the moors towards the radio tower on the distance. When you arrive at the tower cross over and take the same route you came on back to Ravenscar.

- - - o 0 o - - -

ROUTE 8
LEALHOLM RIGG & BROWN RIGG

This is definitely a summer walk as the track over Brown Rigg is very exposed. In winter the cold east winds tear at your flesh as you cross this inhospitable place. However, non of this puts off you serious walkers, does it? The rougher it is the more challenging. Ok then we'll walk the worst part twice to teach you a lesson! The views from Danby Beacon are well worth it and unless you want to return on a busy road there really is no alternative but to walk back the way you came.

20

THE HISTORY

Danby Beacon was used as a tracking station by the RAF, in fact its tracking skills caused the first German plane to be shot down over England. Because of its position men at Danby Beacon had a good view of the surrounding country-side and the skies. The Beacon site was probably used by ancient civilizations for a similar purpose, although all they tracked were Dinosaurs!

INFORMATION

Distance - 13 miles (21km)
Time - 6 hours
Maps - OS Landranger 94. OS Outdoor Leisure 27
Start- Scaling Dam car park GR 755127
Terrain - Moorland paths through heather
Parking - Car park at start
Refreshment - The Board Inn at Lealholm.
There is a tea & sandwich bar in the car park

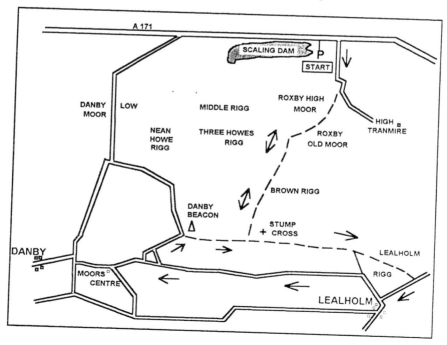

PUT YOUR WOOLLY HAT ON!

Leaving the car park at Scaling Dam off the A171 Whitby to Guisborough road turn right then right again in a few yards at the Tranmire turn off. Shortly leave the road at the bridleway sign on the right and start your ascent of Roxby High Moor on a wide track. This track soon narrows however but there is a path, keep to it. On the horizon on your right you will see Danby Beacon. This track leads you all the way over Brown Rigg to a white road that runs up to the beacon. You join it about ½ mile to the left - so now you know where you are aiming for! At the wide white stony road turn left for a long downhill walk over Lealholm Rigg.

At the tarmac road go right then shortly right again towards Danby, unless you wish to visit the Board Inn at Lealholm which is straight on. The quiet country road twists, turns and climbs for some time with views over Eskdale on the left. Just before the steep downhill turn right and keep right to the site of Danby Beacon which is a good viewpoint. Leave the beacon by the stony road to the right and turn left at the site of Stump Cross to return to the car park on the track on which you came.

--- o 0 o ---

ROUTE 9
ARNSGILL RIDGE & COW RIDGE

This walk takes us almost into Cleveland to the northern extremity of the North York Moors to walk a couple of ridges around Bilsdale. Bilsdale is a sparsley populated valley of great beauty. It is surrounded by riggs and ridges as well as small, peculiar shaped hills. An immense feeling of undisturbed tranquility pervades the vale which is magnified as you ascend the adjacent hills. This walk is pure scenic pleasure!

THE HISTORY

Bilsdale, beautiful Bilsdale. Once a little known valley enclosed by steep hills and wild moorland was first introduced to farming in earnest by the Cistercian Monks. The wool trade was the mainstay of their Abbey and the Brothers developed the valley and the surrounding moors to this end. After the dissolution of the monasteries iron-ore deposits were mined and smelted. In fact a Smith in the valley was mining and smelting his own ore as recent as 1900. Other industries to bloom were Jet and Coal Mining, but the basic economy of Bilsdale has always been and still is farming. The hills and moors surrounding

Bilsdale top out at over 1300ft giving the valley shelter from the cold east winds.. The walk onto Arnsgill Ridge and over Cow Ridge has the most astounding views of Bilsdale, the Hambleton Hills and the unusually shaped hills around Clay Bank. If you look carefully you will be able to see the Wainstones precariously perched on the edge of Broughton Bank. Wherever you look you will find amazing scenery making this one of the most delightful walks in the National Park.

INFORMATION

Distance - 7 miles (11km)
Time - 3½ hours
Maps - OS Landranger 100. OS Outdoor Leisure 26
Start- Chop Gate car park. GR 559994
Terrain - Grass and clay tracks
Parking - Car park at start with toilets
Refreshment -A few yards from the car park is the Sun Inn

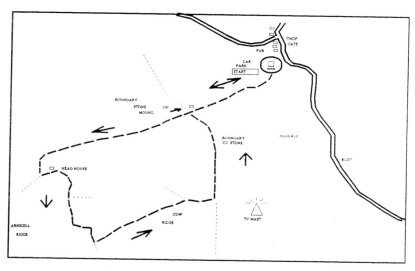

BINOCULARS OUT!

The start of the walk is from the rear of the car park. There are two footpaths there so make sure you leave on the correct one which is over the wooden bridge near the toilets. Cross the bridge and walk along a wide farm road.

Cross the stile then follow the track around to the right then almost immediately left up a grassy slope as directed by a footpath sign on your right. Keep to the edge of the gorge on the left dropping into the gully later on. Soon leave the gully heading for two old stone gateposts on the right with a footpath sign passing through them keeping straight ahead up the hill. Dropping back into the gully cross the stile and keep straight ahead as the gradient becomes more severe. Pass over more stiles and climb up the end of Trennet Bank. At the top keep on the obvious path across the moor eventually reaching the summit where you will find a mound with a cairn and boundary stone on top.

In a few yards cross a wide moorland road to enter a narrow track opposite through the heather. This takes you down hill now to a beck and up the other side heading for the stone enclosure ahead. Pass between the stone walls and the forest to soon meet a wider track. Left here to pass in front of Head House, now used as a shooting lodge. The track now falls and rises again as it crosses the end of Arnsgill Ridge. Keep on this track passing a rough junction on the left. Keep on the wide track for some time until you meet an obvious wide track on the left coming in at an acute angle. Turn along here heading towards Bilsdale TV transmitter. This is Cow Ridge. At the 'T' keep right then join a wide track and turn left onto it. It is a long pull up this track but eventually you reach the mound and marker stone that you passed on the outward journey. Turn right here to return on the track on which you came.

- - - o 0 o - - -

ROUTE 10

PARK RIGG & RANDY RIGG

The Romans were masters at road building and this section across Wheeldale Moor is no exception. In fact it is one of the best preserved Roman roads in the country, although the stones are a bit haphazard now. Could the folk tale that a giant Wade and his wife Bell built the road be true? It would fit in well with many tales of this giant in the area, but I think I'll give credit to the Romans this time.

THE HISTORY

The Roman Road on Wheeldale Moor with its drainage ditches is a monument to the Roman arterial system. It is known as 'Wade's Causeway' and is part of the road from Malton to the coast at Goldsborough. To enable their soldiers to travel quickly they built the roads which were made of stone. When you look at the road don't forget it is thousands of years old! The road also served the

Roman training camp at Cawthorne near Pickering, The coast was important to the Romans as they expected an invasion from the sea. They built a series of signal stations along the high cliffs of the Yorkshire coast to give themselves early warning of any invaders.

High Moor is a haven for birds, look out for Curlew, Snipe and Red Grouse as you navigate your way across. The upper reaches of West Beck from the Mallyan Spout are superb, with the beck bouncing over large rocks through a narrow gorge. The terrain does present some difficulty to walkers though, especially if the beck is in flood.

INFORMATION

Distance - 8½ miles (14 km).

Time - 3½ hours

Map - OS Landranger 94. OS Outdoor Leisure 27

Start - Parking area near Hunt House 2½ miles from Goathland, GR 814989

Terrain - Moorland paths sometimes overgrown with heather, riverside path from Mallyan Spout strenuous when clambering over rocks

Parking - There is roadside parking for 10 cars near Hunt House. It does get filled up quickly in summer so make an early start. Please do not obstruct the road or turning area.

Refreshment - There is a quaint hostelry, the Birch Hall Inn at Beck Hole.Try their excellent ale and 'doorstep' sandwiches. There is a cafe, pub, hotels and shops in Goathland.

MAPS OUT!

Parking is at a premium around Goathland and it pays to make an early start. There is roadside parking at our selected site for about ten cars, please keep off the road and do not park in the turning area. Head off towards the YHA past Hunt House following the sign for 'Roman Road via stepping stones 1.5 miles'. Continue past the YHA to a sign which directs you right over a stile to the Roman Road across Wheeldale Beck. It is a stiff climb onto Wheeldale Moor but the path soon flattens out. At the Roman Road turn right to a gate and large stile. Over the stile keep close to the wall on the right to another stile in the corner of the field. Take the wide track to the left now passing a footpath sign half way down. At Wheeldale Gill go right over a stile then follow the Gill around to the left and cross the first wooden bridge. Left again following the

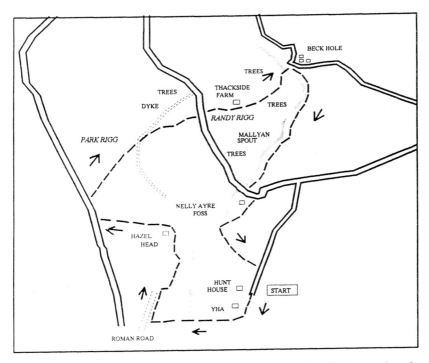

bridleway arrow to a gate marked as 'Right of Way'. Climb up the slope passing through two gates bearing right still following the blue bridleway arrows.

At Hazel Head farm follow the blue arrow through the farmyard to exit by the gate opposite. Do not go through the next gate but turn left following the footpath sign. There is an odd stile here which is freestanding, there is nothing attached to either side of it! The path leads to a wider track and shortly over a stile onto the moor. Follow the path to the road and in ½ mile turn right onto High Moor at a metal bridleway sign. The track over the moor is narrow and sometimes overgrown, head for the solitary tree on the horizon if in doubt. Park Dyke eventually runs along our route, keep close to this and it will lead you, not without difficulty, to the edge of the moor. Where the path leaves the moor there is a wire fence. Follow it left to the stone wall then take the path between the fence and the wall which leads to a stile to the right into a field. Continue slightly right across the field to a gate opposite with a blue bridleway arrow. Go through the gate and descend left through a pretty wood. At the bottom follow the sign going right then left to meet the road. Cross the road taking the bridleway along the road to Thackside Farm. Cross another stile following the signs past the farm eventually picking up a blue bridleway arrow signed to Beck Hole. Keep following the bridleway signs until you reach a small gate into a wood. Keep following the blue bridleway arrows through the wood until you meet a sign giving you a choice of route to Beck Hole. Take the yellow arrow to the right, over the river and a stile then through a gate towards Beck Hole. If you do not wish to visit Beck Hole go right at the sign for Goathland then right through a gate 'To The Mallyan' opposite Incline Cottage. Follow the track to the river and at the signpost keep straight on for Mallyan Spout a superb waterfall. The river walk is sometimes tiresome and ends at a road. Left here and up the hill, ignore the bridleway sign but take the footpath sign to the right signed to Nelly Aire Foss. This wide path leads gently upward to meet the road, at the road go right and in about a mile you will return to the parking area near Hunt House.

- - - o O o - - -

ROUTE 11
SIX RIGGS & A RIDGE AROUND GOATHLAND

Goathland is surrounded by moors and Riggs. Heading off across Whinstone Ridge we climb over York Cross Rigg and Foster Howes Rigg to reach Lilla Rigg. The return route uses part of the long distance Lyke Wake Walk over Lilla Rigg and Crag Stone Rigg. Turning back to Goathland at Simon Howe Rigg over Two Howes Rigg to descend past a pretty tarn on the way.

THE HISTORY

Goathland, or Gothland as it was called is at the centre of this walk. A Goth is described as a 'barbarous person' so Gothland might have been the land or place of the Goths! Surely there were many such people around the North York Moors hundreds of years ago, let us hope we don't meet any of their ancestors! Whinstone Ridge is a solidified lava flow from 50 or so million years ago. It is known as the Cleveland Dyke and has been mined and quarried for use in road building. You will see much evidence of this further north. York Cross, seems to be two different parts as the base and the shaft do not look to have aged at the same rate. There are many ancient tracks and old pannierways in this area when all transport was either on foot or pulled or carried by the horse. Many were paved, they represented the motorways of their day!

INFORMATION

Distance - 12 miles (19km)
Time - 5 hours
Map - OS Landranger 94
OS Outdoor Leisure 27
Start - Goathland. GR 833013
Terrain - Moorland tracks, sometimes boggy
Parking - Small car park in Goathland
Refreshments - Cafes and pubs in Goathland

DON'T FORGET YOUR SANDWICHES!

From the village car park turn left away from the shops and towards the railway station. Go down the hill to the station and cross the railway track with care. At the other side go straight ahead up a steep bank onto the moor keeping straight ahead to eventually meet a tarn. Go right of the tarn and head diagonally to the right on a sometimes undefined track through the heather to soon meet the road. Left here to climb the hill, at the top at the Green End/Beck Hole junction go across the rough car park on the right to meet the main road in a few yards. Cross the busy road with care to enter the moor through a gate opposite. Follow the track bearing to the right as it climbs across Whinstone Ridge and York Cross Rigg. Continue climbing across Foster Howes Rigg and

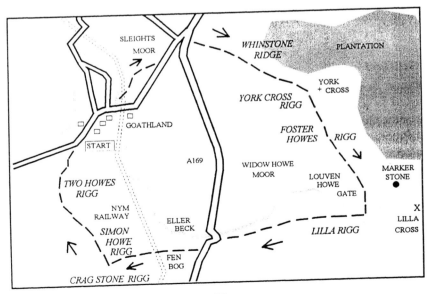

past Ann's Cross keeping to the left of the fence. It is quite a pull to the top of the moor, when you reach the gate go through it bearing right and walk down the hill onto Lilla Rigg. Lilla Cross is on the left in the distance if you wish to make a detour. When a wide track meets on the left turn along it to pick up the odd sign for the Lyke Wake Walk (LWW). Keep well to the right of the danger area signs heading down the hill to eventually meet the road at Eller Beck.

Cross the busy road turning left then almost immediately right onto a wide, rough car park. Continue straight ahead through the rough area and straight on to the track to Fen Bog, a nature reserve. Cross the railway track where indicated and head straight up the hill onto a wide track climbing for some time over Cragg Stone Rigg to reach Simon Howe and its Rigg. Turn right at the Howe and follow a path onto Two Howes Rigg. The Two Howes you will soon see in the distance straight ahead. Aim for the two howes and pass them on the left down a stony track to a tarn. After a rest by the tarn bear right of it and make your way over a small hill then down to the road. Turn right onto the road then left at the junction. In about half a mile turn right past the shops to the car park.

- - - o 0 o - - -

ROUTE 12
ELM RIDGE

Elm Ridge is situated adjacent to the moorland village of Lealholm. It is only a small ridge and the walk to it is short, perhaps it should be attempted on the way home from walking another Ridge or Rigg in the area. It is worthy of inclusion in the book for the superb views along Eskdale to Danby Castle in the west and south to the lush Great Fryup Dale and Glaisdale Rigg.

THE HISTORY
The village of Lealholm is picturesque in itself. The River Esk flowing through the village with stepping stones on which to cross to the opposite bank. There is a Garden Centre and a Craft Shop as well as a restaurant and a pub. The Esk Valley railway passes through the village of Lealholm stopping at the station on its way to Middlesbrough or Whitby, alas it is infrequently used and is always under threat of closure. There is an old methodist Chapel which is over 150 years old and has the high flood water marks on the wall of the building. There is a free car park and toilets.

INFORMATION

Distance - 2 miles (3 km)
Time - 1 hour
Maps - OS Landranger 94. OS Outdoor Leisure 27
Start- Lealholm. GR 763077
Terrain- Easy grassy path and farm track
Parking- Free car park in village with toilets
Refreshment -The Board Inn. The Shepherds Hall Restaurant

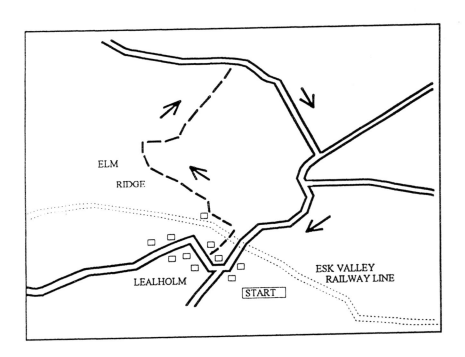

WATCH OUT FOR TRAINS!

From the car park go left then immediately right and walk in the direction of Danby. At the post office bear right at the public footpath sign along an uphill driveway. Cross the railway where indicated by a white gate and a yellow waymark. Bear left over the railway towards the station house. Bear right here up to a waymarked gate into a field. Climb up onto Elm Ridge for marvellous views across Eskdale and Great Fryup Dale. You can return the same way but if you wish to make a circular walk of it continue along the ridge to another gate. Do not go through the gate but turn right following the waymark to a group of signposts across the field. Turn right here signed 'Footpath to Waymark 2' then soon down a short but steep bank onto a farm track. Continue straight ahead along the track. Turn left off this track to cross a stream and shortly join a farm road. Turn right onto the farm road which takes you to the road. At the road turn right to return to Lealholm.

- - - o 0 o - - -

PUBLICATIONS BY THE SAME AUTHOR
Walking around the North York Moors
Walking on the Yorkshire Coast
Walking to Abbeys, Castles & Churches
Short Walks around the Yorkshire Coast
- - - o 0 o - --
Mountain Biking around the Yorkshire Dales
Mountain Biking The Easy Way
Mountain Biking in North Yorkshire
Mountain Biking on the Yorkshire Wolds
Mountain Biking around Ryedale, Wydale & North York Moors
Beadle's Bash, 100 mile Mountain Bike Route
On The Ruffstuff - 84 mountain bike rides across the North of England

- - - o 0 o - - -

IN THE POCKETBOOK SERIES
The Crucial Guide to the Yorkshire Coast
The Crucial Guide to Ryedale & North York Moors

Tourist Information Centres

Bridlington, 25 Prince Street	01262 673474
Danby Moors Centre, Danby.	01287 660308
Filey, John Street	01723 512204
Guisborough, Priory Grounds	01287 633801
Helmsley, Market Place.	01439 770173
Malton, 58 Market Square	01653 600048
Middlesbrough, 51 Corporation Road	01642 243425
Pickering, Eastgate Car Park	01751 473791
Saltburn, Station Square	01287 622422
Scarborough, St.Nicholas Cliff	01723 373333
Sutton Bank, Car Park	01845 597426
Whitby, Langbourne Road	01947 602674

RIGHTS OF WAY

- BRIDLEWAYS - (Blue markings) Open to cyclist, walkers and horses.
- BYWAYS - (Red markings) Open to cyclists, walkers, horses and some traffic.
- PUBLIC FOOTPATHS - (Yellow markings) Walkers only.
- OPEN LAND - Moorland, farmland etc. No right of access unless permission from landowner is obtained.
- TOWPATHS - Some are available for cycling without restriction, some are not. Others need a cycling permit available form British Waterways.
- PAVEMENTS - Walkers only.
- CYCLE PATHS - Information availabe from Borough and County Councils.